C000129679

THE ORIGINAL

THE CAT

Artist Collection

THIS IS A CARLTON BOOK

The Cat Logos and Photographs © 2005
artlist INTERNATIONAL
Design copyright © 2005 Carlton Books
Limited
Text copyright © 2005 Rod Green

This edition published in 2005 by
Carlton Books Ltd
A Division of the Carlton Publishing Group
20 Mortimer Street
London
W1T 3JW

A CIP catalogue record for this book is
available from the British Library.

ISBN 1 84442 476 6

Executive Editor: Amie McKee
Art Director: Clare Baggaley
Design: Michelle Pickering
Production: Claire Hayward

Printed and bound in Singapore by Tien Wah

THE CAT

Artlist Collection

COSY CATS

CARLTON
BOOKS

Abyssinian

Abyssinian

Abyssinian

Abyssinian

Abyssinian

Mixed Breed

Mixed Breed

Mixed Breed

Himalayan

Himalayan

Himalayan

Mixed Breed

Bengal

Bengal

Bengal

Russian Blue

Russian Blue

Russian Blue

Russian Blue

Mixed Breed

Mixed Breed

American Curl

American Curl

American Curl

Mixed Breed

Munchkin

Mixed Breed

Mixed Breed

Singapura

Norwegian Forest Cat

Norwegian Forest Cat

Somali

Somali

Exotic Shorthair

Ocicat

Ocicat

Ragdoll

Mixed Breed

Mixed Breed

Oriental Shorthair

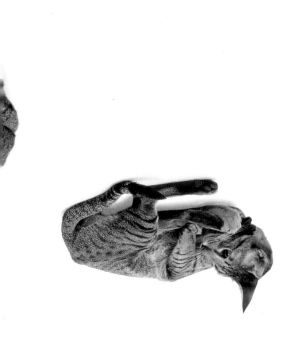

Oriental Shorthair

Persian

Persian

Persian

Persian

Persian

Persian

Burmese

Burmese

American Shorthair

American Shorthair

American Shorthair

Maine Coon

Maine Coon

Maine Coon

Mixed Breed

Siberian Forest Cat

Scottish Fold

Scottish Fold

Scottish Fold